# When We Say 'Hiroshima'

Kurihara Sadako with daughter Mariko, 1937. Courtesy of Kurihara Sadako.

# When We Say 'Hiroshima'

## Selected Poems

### Kurihara Sadako

Translated with an Introduction by
Richard H. Minear

Center for Japanese Studies
The University of Michigan
Ann Arbor, Michigan    1999

Michigan Monograph Series in Japanese Studies, No. 23

Published by the Center for Japanese Studies,
The University of Michigan,
202 S. Thayer St., Ann Arbor, MI 48104–1608

Distributed by The University of Michigan Press,
839 Greene St. / P.O. Box 1104, Ann Arbor, MI 48106–1104

Library of Congress Cataloging in Publication Data
Kurihara, Sadako.
    [Kuroi tamago. English]
    When we say 'Hiroshima' : selected poems / Kurihara Sadako ;
translated with an introduction by Richard H. Minear.
    xv, 57 p. 19 cm.—(Michigan monograph series in Japanese studies ; 23)
    All of the poems appeared originally in the book Black Eggs.
    ISBN 978-0-939512-89-8 (pbk. : alk. paper)
    1. Kurihara, Sadako—Translations into English. 2. Hiroshima-shi
(Japan)—History—Bombardment, 1945—Poetry. 3. Atomic bomb
victims—Japan—Hiroshima-shi—Poetry. I. Minear, Richard H.
II. Title. III. Series.
PL855.U66K8713    1999
895.6'15—dc21                                                    98–31741
                                                                    CIP

Cover design: Seiko Semones
Cover photo: Kurihara Sadako, 1989. Courtesy of *Asahi shimbun*.

This publication meets the ANSI/NISO Standards
for Permanence of Paper for Publications and Documents
in Libraries and Archives (Z39.48–1992).

Printed and bound by CPI Group (UK) Ltd, Croydon, CR0 4YY

# Contents

v

# Translator's Introduction[1]

Kurihara Sadako was born in Hiroshima; she was in Hiroshima on August 6, 1945; and she has lived in Hiroshima ever since. She is a Hiroshima poet, one of the most important poets of the atomic bomb. Yet her poetry is "atomic bomb literature" only in part. It is also poetry of the Pacific War, the nuclear age, and postwar Japan.[2]

Kurihara Sadako is also an activist and a leader of the antinuclear movement in Japan. She composes poems, reads her poems, writes essays, and edits "atomic bomb literature." She also acts: as recently as June 1992 she took part in the campaign against sending Japanese troops abroad under the auspices of the United Nations, and she participated in a sit-in protesting the words of an American delegate to a United Nations conference in Hiroshima. Indeed, her political activities may keep critics from realizing that she is one of postwar Japan's greatest poets.

There are other reasons for the fact that Kurihara the poet is relatively unknown in Japan today: she is a woman; she writes from strong political convictions; she lives in Hiroshima, not Tokyo; and she publishes her poems and essays in journals that are hardly mainstream. Paradoxically, the same factors may contribute to the strength of her poetry.

*****

Kurihara Sadako was born Doi Sadako in Hiroshima city in 1913, second daughter of a farm family. Her formal schooling took place between 1919, when she entered primary school, and 1930, when she graduated from girls' higher school. In terms of the curriculum of today's American schools, her education was perhaps the equivalent of four years of college, but the school itself—run by the prefecture—was hardly an elite institution. Doi Sadako composed her first poems in 1926, when she was thirteen. Her first published poem appeared in Hiroshima's newspaper, *Chūgoku shinbun*, in 1930, when she was seventeen.

At eighteen, Doi Sadako met Kurihara Tadaichi, the man with whom she would spend the next fifty years. Then twenty-five, Tadaichi came from the same village as Sadako, but he had already moved into a larger world. A middle-school dropout, he had thrown himself into leftist politics after the Great Earthquake of 1923. In Tokyo he took part in anarchist meetings. This activity made him a marked man, and when he returned to Hiroshima from Tokyo at the end of the 1920s, he was under police surveillance. Tadaichi and Sadako ran away from Hiroshima, going by boat to Matsuyama on Shikoku. However, they soon ran out of money, and on their return to Hiroshima, the police picked her up and returned her to her family. Though they treated their daughter with kindness, her family would not countenance Tadaichi. But Sadako and Tadaichi soon got back together, and they lived in Osaka, Tokushima, and Matsuyama before economic hardship drove them back to Hiroshima.[3]

Their first child was born in poverty in 1932, when Sadako was 19. That child, their only son, died of malnutrition in 1934. Daughters followed: Mariko in 1935 and Junko in 1939. In 1931 Kurihara's parents had cut off relations with her in protest against her marriage to Tadaichi, but relations resumed on the birth of her second daughter in 1939.

Between 1937 and 1944, the Kuriharas ran a kitchen-goods store in Hiroshima, but they shared a life on the home front that was never good and soon got worse. In 1944 wartime shortages meant no goods to sell, and Tadaichi and Sadako eventually closed the store.

During the war Sadako was on call to neighborhood mobilizations for work gangs and air-raid drills. On August 5, 1945, the day before the bomb, she worked clearing firebreaks in Tenjin-chō, close to ground zero. On August 6, 1945, she was at home, 2.5 miles from ground zero. "The Day of the Atomic Bomb" speaks with riveting intensity of her experience that day, and many other poems deal with her experience of the aftermath of the bomb.

*****

After the war Kurihara Sadako involved herself in literary and political activities. Tadaichi ran for political office and was elected to Hiroshima's prefectural assembly in 1955, serving three terms (twelve years), and Sadako played an important role in many of his political activities. She also became increasingly involved in issues of national and international political import. She wrote poems in support of the movement against the U.S.-Japan Security Treaty (1960), poems attacking U.S. policy in Vietnam, and poems attacking nuclear power in Japan and around the world (Three Mile Island, Chernobyl). She took on Japanese politicians of the conservative mainstream, from mayors of Hiroshima to prime ministers to the emperor, and she fought against the resurgence of nationalism and the de facto Japanese national flag, the *Hinomaru*.

The major early survivor-writers of Hiroshima's atomic experience died much too early: Hara Tamiki, by suicide, in 1951; Tōge Sankichi in 1953; Ōta Yōko in 1963; and Shōda Shinoe in 1965. That left Kurihara Sadako and a few others such as the poet Ōhara Miyao (1905–92) and the critic Nagaoka Hiroyoshi (d. 1989) to carry on. Thirty-two years old when the bomb fell, Sadako was eighty-two when, in 1995, the world commemorated August 6, 1945 for the fiftieth time.

Particularly after 1965, Kurihara stressed Japan's role as victimizer in the Pacific War. The poem for which she is most famous today outside of Japan, "When We Say 'Hiroshima'" (May 1972), speaks eloquently on the score of Japan as victimizer. It is perhaps symbolic of the Japanese scene until very recently that Kurihara is known in Japan most widely not for this poem but for the relatively apolitical "Let Us Be Midwives!"

Kurihara's political engagement included reaching out to the international peace community in prose and poetry, defending atomic bomb literature and its writers against hostile critics, and drawing parallels between atomic bomb literature and the literature of the European holocaust. Political engagement also meant choices that left Kurihara at odds with former allies. For example, in 1961 the Soviet Union resumed nuclear testing. Japanese antinuclear groups, overwhelmingly leftist in orientation, had to decide whether to indict the Soviet Union in the same terms that they had used for the United States. Kurihara was a member of a group of women artists who decided to attack all nuclear testing. As Kurihara wrote in an essay of 1980: "Contamination of the environment and damage to the human body are the same no matter whether the country exploding the bomb is capitalist or socialist."[4] That decision left her an outcast. Yet she has continued to be an activist to this day, despite a serious traffic accident in 1994 that left her unable to walk.

In 1990 Kurihara was awarded the third Tanimoto Kiyoshi Prize. (Tanimoto was the Methodist minister who figures so prominently in John Hersey's *Hiroshima*.) Her acceptance speech on November 24th of that year was typical: little about herself, much about issues. In the second half of her speech she criticized those in Japan who would portray Japan as a victim but not victimizer:

> The dropping of the atomic bomb, a crime against international law, is intolerable. But flat-out denying historical fact—saying that there was no rape of Nanking, that the Chinese dreamed it up—and then on top of that bringing in America's dropping of the atomic bomb in order to absolve Japan of guilt as victimizer: that is to use Japan's *hibakusha* [atomic bomb victims] to advance one's argument through sheer force. The *hibakusha* of Hiroshima and Nagasaki are mortified. . . .
>
> Until now, *hibakusha* of Hiroshima and Nagasaki have gone abroad to argue the cruelty of atomic bombs and to plead for the abolition of nuclear weapons, but recently victims of the war have begun to come to Japan from Asia and the Pacific to testify to the large-scale atrocities that the Japanese army committed. . . .
>
> Hiroshima was once Fortress Hiroshima, and today it maintains throughout the city imposing cenotaphs and ruins in memory of emperors and their army; these monuments sing of holy war. Hiroshima itself was a victim, of course, but the true Hiroshima demands an acknowledgment of Japan's war guilt and a sensitivity to the aggression and murder Japan committed. Failure on these fronts raises questions about Japan's war guilt and about its militarization as a great power since. The true Hiroshima demands that there be

a "dual awareness, of Japan as victim and Japan
as victimizer."

*****

As Kurihara stated in 1985: "Literature is not dependent upon
politics; it goes ahead of politics. In every age free literature
stands in opposition to the status quo."[5] Kurihara plays im-
portant editorial and political roles in preserving and defend-
ing the heritage of Hiroshima literature and poetry, but she
is not primarily a literary critic. She is a poet, composer of
some four hundred poems, and author of over one hundred
essays. For Kurihara, to live is to write poetry. Kurihara's po-
ems and essays have won her an audience, but in the most
basic sense she writes for herself. Kurihara defended Hara
Tamiki's right to be left in peace and Ōta Yōko's right to stop
addressing the issues of the atomic bomb, but Kurihara's in-
domitable spirit would not let her forsake Hiroshima and the
bomb. Nor could she be persuaded by Ōe Kenzaburō's *Hiro-
shima Notes* that suicide is a legitimate way out. Thus does
Kurihara reveal her own toughness and devotion to life.

Kurihara's life is an act of faith in words, but words
themselves are not the goal. As she writes in the Introduc-
tion to *Kuroi tamago* ("Black Eggs," 1946), poetry is not "the
depiction of simple sensual beauty, self-complacent emotional
pain, and dark melancholy—things not real mirrored in mor-
bid sensibilities."[6] Poems are words, but the key element is
the "unity of ideas" that must undergird the poems. That is,
the beauty and force of poetry must be harnessed to ideas,
and the ideas must suit the times. For Kurihara, the ideas are
those of "a new humanism," and she listens intently for its
footsteps. To be sure, this is Kurihara at her most didactic;
usually she lets her poems themselves be the focus.

As Kurihara herself has written, there are striking
parallels between Hiroshima literature and the literature of

the European Holocaust. Both are literatures *in extremis*; both are literatures of witness. Here is a comment from 1985: "Atomic bomb poetry and prose began to be written by novelists, poets, and anonymous individuals who experienced firsthand being speechless, able only to stand dumb in the midst of mass death—written because as human beings they could not not speak of it."[7]

*****

For the past dozen years I have studied the literature of Hiroshima. I began my study of Kurihara's poetry by translating the poems that dealt with the atomic bomb. But as I worked my way into the world of Kurihara's poetry, I was struck with its breadth and depth and beauty. I realized also how different it is from what the prevailing stereotypes lead us to expect. Further, I saw how far Kurihara's world is from the world of those on whom Japanese and American critics alike have focused their attention.

Kurihara lives in the nuclear age: "The human alienation of nukes and pollution is the very essence of the nuclear age; it is the end phase of a modern science and culture that are contemptuous of people and treat them as objects." She strives to universalize the *hibakusha* experience and make of it a fundamental element of modern thought, to use it in the cause of human liberation from things nuclear. Thus, Hiroshima and Nagasaki become an indispensable part of today's ideas, part not of the past but of the future:

> Hiroshima is by no means something that happened in the past. As the cruelest end point of Fortress Hiroshima, Hiroshima is a futurescape in which we see where militarism leads, where the arms race leads, their destination; it is humankind's greatest blind spot that serves notice to the world.[8]

In conditions ranging from censorship to relative toleration, over not twenty-five years but more than fifty, with a persistence and application only the mural painters Maruki Iri (1901–96) and Maruki Toshi (1912– ) can equal, Kurihara Sadako has kept the faith. In the process, she has produced a body of poetry that will surely stand as one of the major artistic testimonies to life in the nuclear age.

*****

The selection and arrangement—partly aesthetic and partly (within each of the two sections) chronological—of the poems in this book are the result of collaboration between the translator and the poet Sarah Messer. Indeed, this book itself is Sarah's idea. I acknowledge her crucial role and thank her most sincerely. Bruce Willoughby of the Center for Japanese Studies played again the role he played in the publication of *Black Eggs*. Translators and authors in search of a supportive yet assertive editor can hardly go wrong with Bruce and the Center.

## Notes

1. For a fuller introduction to Kurihara's life and work, see the "Translator's Introduction" in Kurihara Sadako, *Black Eggs*, trans. and ed. Richard H. Minear (Ann Arbor: Center for Japanese Studies, The University of Michigan, 1994), 1–38. Japanese names are presented in Japanese order, with surnames first.
2. For biographical data on Kurihara see the chronology in Kurihara Sadako, *Kurihara Sadako shishū* [Poems of Kurihara Sadako], Nihon gendaishi bunko 17 (Tokyo: Doyō Bijutsusha, 1984), 155–60, and a series of sixteen brief articles (unsigned) in Hiroshima's *Chūgoku shinbun* beginning July 17, 1987.
3. *Chūgoku shinbun*, July 17, 1987. The chronology in *Kurihara Sadako shishū* gives December 26, 1931, as the date of her "marriage," but in a later essay Kurihara writes of an "illegal marriage" at the end of 1931. See "Sensō to kakumeiteki romanchishizumu no hazama de" [Caught between war and revolutionary romanticism] (Au-

gust 1990), in *Towareru Hiroshima* [Questions for Hiroshima] (Tokyo: San'ichi, 1992), 153–54.

4. "Hankaku ishiki no saikōchiku o—daiikkai genbaku mondai sōgō kenkyūkai no kiroku" [Toward the reconstitution of antinuclear consciousness—record of the first meeting of the general study group on the atomic bomb issue], in *Kaku jidai ni ikiru* [Living in the nuclear age] (Tokyo: San'ichi, 1982), 228.

5. *Chūgoku shinbun*, October 26, 1985.

6. "Introduction," in Kurihara, *Black Eggs*, 45.

7. *Chūgoku shinbun*, October 19, 1985.

8. "Genten to genten" [Where we began and where we are today] (August 15, 1973), in *Hiroshima no genfūkei o idaite* [Embracing the atomic landscape of Hiroshima] (Tokyo: Miraisha, 1975), 186; "Atogaki: kaku to tennō no zettaisei kara no kaihō o" [Afterword: toward liberation from the absolutism of nukes and the emperor] (March 1978), in *Kaku, tennō, hibakusha* [Nukes, emperor, *hibakusha*] (Tokyo: San'ichi, 1978), 229; "Genbaku ireihi to Yasukuni jinja" [The atomic cenotaph and Yasukuni shrine] (July 1974), in *Hiroshima no genfūkei o idaite*, 242.

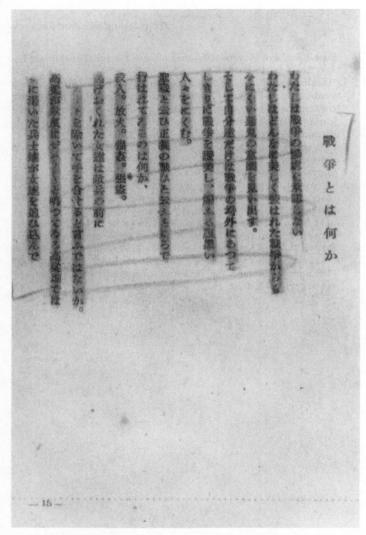

In 1946 Kurihara submitted page proofs of *Kuroi tamago* ("Black Eggs") for prepublication censorship to the American Occupation. This photograph, of page 15 of those proofs, shows what the censors did to "War: What Is It?" The title is at the right, not crossed out. Courtesy of the Gordon W. Prange Collection, University of Maryland College Park Libraries.

# Part One

The dates and occasional notes to the poems from *Kuroi tamago* ("Black Eggs") were not part of the first (1946) edition; the poet added them to the complete edition of 1983. This translation gives month and year but not day. All notes are the poet's except for those that begin with the translator's initials, RHM.

# Part One

## SACHIKO, DEAD IN THE ATOMIC BOMBING

Iwojima fell,
Okinawa fought to the last man—
not even empty funerary urns came back,
cities throughout the land were burned to blackened waste,
and then
August sixth, 1945:
blue sky perfectly still.
Air-raid hood of padded cotton
over your shoulder,
you were mobilized to raze buildings
        for the forced evacuations—

suddenly,
the blue flash:
buildings collapse,
fires blaze,
and amid swirling smoke
hordes of people in flight
thread their way through downed wires.

On the evening of the third day
we brought your corpse home.
A dark night: air-raid alarm
that was never lifted.
In the black night Hiroshima burned red.
The eve of the surrender,
all Japan as if holding vigil.
A dark room sealed off by blackout curtains.
You laid out before the *butsudan*,
a white handkerchief over your face.

In the dusk at the aid station
crazed victims
had shouted like wild animals
and raced about the classrooms;
grotesquely swollen, people with burns had groaned
and given off alive the stench of death.
The corpses were lined up like so many heaps of rags
on the dirt floor of Koi Primary School,
and we knew you only by your metal ID.
Over your face—
a white handkerchief
someone had placed there.
The handkerchief was stuck fast to your burns
and would not come off.

A junior in girls' higher school,
not understanding what the war was about,
you died, Sachiko, before you could blossom.
Your mother
draped a brand-new gown,
white and flowered,
over the school uniform burned to tatters
and seared onto your skin.
"I made it for you, but because of the war,
you never got to wear it."
Her arms around you, she broke down and wept.

—AUGUST 1946

RHM: A *butsudan* is a Buddhist altar in a private home. Koi was then a suburb of Hiroshima, at the foot of the hills immediately to the west of the city.

## LET US BE MIDWIVES!

### —An untold story of the atomic bombing

Night in the basement of a concrete structure now in ruins.
Victims of the atomic bomb
jammed the room;
it was dark—not even a single candle.
The smell of fresh blood, the stench of death,
    the closeness of sweaty people, the moans.
From out of all that, lo and behold, a voice:
"The baby's coming!"
In that hellish basement, at that very moment,
a young woman had gone into labor.
In the dark, without a single match, what to do?
People forgot their own pains, worried about her.
And then: "I'm a midwife. I'll help with the birth."
The speaker, seriously injured herself,
    had been moaning only moments before.
And so new life was born in the dark of that pit of hell.
And so the midwife died before dawn, still bathed in blood.
Let us be midwives!
Let us be midwives!
Even if we lay down our own lives to do so.

—SEPTEMBER 1945

This poem appeared first in the inaugural issue of *Chūgoku bunka* (the special issue on the atomic bomb, March 1946). The cellar in the poem was the cellar of the old post office in Senda-machi.

## CITY UNDER GROUND

Like a keloid hand opened out,
seven rivers flow, full of the water of agony.
Under the city in the delta,
the burned corpses of August still lie, tightly compacted.
Now, as then, roasted by broiling sand and sun,
now, as then, fallen in heaps in burning streetcars,
now, as then, burned hands holding tight to burned hands,
now, as then, heaped like trash on the concrete floor
    of a dark aid station,
now, as then, pinned beneath heavy beams—
not yet humus,
they form instead
a mushy human mud.

Finally covered over, the city under ground
will become a layer of rubble and bones,
the twentieth century's
atomic stratum.
It will bring a gleam to the eyes
of archeologists—
"Hiroshima: that was a civilization!"

—AUGUST 1952

# CITY RAVAGED BY FLAMES

## (1)

City of rubble
ravaged by flames:
wind blows
restlessly;
has autumn deepened?

Amid rubble
ravaged by flames,
stand shacks
here and there;
smoke rises.

Shacks with roofs
of burnt tin:
a cold late-autumn shower
wets them
and passes on.

Vermilion
bright as ever,
a fire pumper
lies on its side in a street
ravaged by flames.

Houses
where wives, children, relatives
lived happily:
all now
rubble.

7

Amid rubble
ravaged by flames,
the last moments
of thousands:
what sadness!

Thousands of people,
tens of thousands:
lost
the instant
the bomb exploded.

Silent, all sorrows
unspoken,
city of rubble
ravaged by flames:
autumn rain falls.

**(2)**

In a garden
ravaged by flames,
four o'clocks
blossom in silence;
I see no one.

Amid rubble
ravaged by flames,
morning glories bloom,
wet with dew;
yes, winter is near.

Amid rubble
ravaged by flames,

8

a single blue mustard
leafs out
in such profusion.

The bark of trees
ravaged by flames
is sooty;
branches
send out shoots.

Shacktown
ravaged by flames:
each shack
has its garden,
already green.

### (3)

Autumn drizzle stops,
starts again:
winter cold has come
to shacks
ravaged by flames.

Inside,
wood-chip fires burn
brightly, brightly:
families gathered
for supper.

Burned rust-red,
metal pots
roll about;
rays of the setting sun fall
on this city of rubble.

9

City of rubble
ravaged by flames:
at dusk
I hear cries
from the world of the dead.

City of rubble
ravaged by flames:
walk alone,
and you're
not really alone.

Pine grove
where the wind
once sighed:
only trunks remain,
burned black.

—OCTOBER 1945

Part 1 was composed on the way to Ushita, on the twelfth, and part 2 was composed on the twenty-seventh. Part 3 is set in the pine grove at Izumi Mansion.

10

## ON A DAY OF POWDERY SNOW

A cold wind blows fiercely; a powdery snow falls.
I go out in search of underwear to buy
and, pleased with myself, return with a quick step.
And then up ahead, a single line approaches
    at a solemn pace,
the man in front carrying a white box chest high.
Did this brave soldier die fighting in the South?
Did he die fighting in the North?
My eyes go hot, tears form, I bow my head
    in a moment of prayer.
The package of underwear is in my hand,
but my pleasure has turned hollow.
A cold wind blows fiercely; a powdery snow falls.

—January 1943

11

## THE FOX'S GOLD COINS

My heart is lonely and sealed off,
it tries to converse with no one.
Not a single person speaks any more
of life in all its freshness and reality.
People are fanatic about the war,
and the world has become a vast insane asylum.
Thrust sane into its midst,
I am lost.
When from time to time I let slip a sigh,
it is a poor mother whose son died in battle
who sends me a sad glance and a "me too."
Raving lunatics laugh aloud
even when sons and husbands die in battle,
boast of silly Orders of the Golden Kite—
gold coins from a fox,
and venerate their dead as gods.
Hereabouts
this is the highest virtue.

—AUGUST 1942

RHM: The Order of the Golden Kite was awarded for outstanding valor to
servicemen or their survivors. A golden kite had perched on the bow of
Emperor Jinmu, the legendary conqueror who led the march eastward into
Yamato. See also "The Day the Shōwa Era Ends" (below). In Japanese
folklore, foxes caught by humans often buy their freedom by offering their
captors gold coins. However, the gold soon turns into worthless leaves (one
standard gold coin was called a "leaf").

## WHAT IS WAR?

I do not accept war's cruelty.
In every war, no matter how beautifully dressed up,
I detect ugly, demonic intent.
And I abhor those blackhearted people
who, not involved directly themselves,
constantly glorify war and fan its flames.
What is it that takes place
when people say "holy war," "just war"?
Murder. Arson. Rape. Theft.
The women who can't flee take off their skirts
    before the enemy troops
and beg for mercy—do they not?
In fields where the grain rustles in the breeze,
sex-starved soldiers chase the women,
like demons on the loose.
At home they are good fathers, good brothers, good sons,
but in the hell of battle,
they lose all humanity
and rampage like wild beasts.

—OCTOBER 1942

This poem was censored in its entirety by SCAP in 1946.

13

## RESPECT FOR HUMANITY

They denounced us
for being
too materialistic;
but what of their
"human resources"?

"It's state policy,
so have children!"
Sounds as easy as
getting hens
to lay more eggs.

"It's state policy,
so have children!"
In the end,
respect for life
gets trampled.

Goods for consumption
twenty years later—
women, get angry
at systematized
life and death!

Militarism
is an abomination;
women of the world—
until it dies,
don't have children!

The old soldier, too,
beaten
with a horse whip
for not
saluting.

In 1941 the Ministry of Public Welfare established a wartime population policy, based on Nazi ideas of eugenics, prohibiting contraception and abortion; in the postwar era of shortages of housing and food, it lifted the prohibition on abortion. This is the basis of the current Eugenics Protection Act. The movement to "amend" the Eugenics Protection Act that has recently [1983] become controversial can be described as aiming at a reversion to the prewar system.

15

## RUINS

Hiroshima: nothing, nothing—
old and young burned to death,
city blown away,
socket without an eyeball.
White bones scattered over reddish rubble;
above, sun burning down:
city of ruins, still as death.
Look: on my sleeve, my shoulder,
covering every last inch—
yes, a swarm of black flies!
Bred in the pulpy entrails and putrid flesh
of our dead,
white larvae grow fat on bloody pus,
cling to the rubble.
Shoo, fly! Shoo, fly! But they don't shoo.
They swarm over clothes, attached almost.

Seven years have passed, and even today the flies
buzz all over, spreading invisible bacteria.
The busy square in front of the station.
Wearing khaki, the Police Reserve is everywhere;
the smell of leather is strong.

Ever since being hit that day
by a blast fierce enough to blow away the globe,
this city has lost everything.
Though the world outside is angry enough to burst,

16

this city's people are silent, exactly as silent
as the ruins on August sixth.

—AUGUST 1952

RHM: The National Police Reserve (1950–52) was one of two predecessors
of the Self-Defense Forces, established in 1954. The line about the silence of
the *hibakusha* may surprise the reader, but it was many years after the war
before the dropping of the bomb became a political issue, and many *hiba-
kusha* remained silent their entire lives.

## RECONSTRUCTION

Insides hollow, windows blown out in the blast,
mouths gaping idiotically,
the great buildings are like people done in
    by the tragedy of the century.
Their trunks a forlorn row, the black trees
    that survived the flames
sing a weird song of death,
and the rubble still holds horror and the stench of death.

To this city—
has time passed so quickly?—
those who fled that day's horrible hell
to villages in the hills return,
recovered in body if not in soul,
and build small huts.

With child, spouse, mother dead,
who needs a large house?
In the small shacks
the survivors call constantly, "Come closer,"
keep each other warm, and carry on.

Day by day, the shacks grow in number, and land
    thought barren—
it too is leveled nicely and soon green with vegetables.
Here and there even now people raise small ridgepoles
    and build houses.

The houses are crude, like those the first humans built
    in the virgin forest,
but these people show even more resolute strength
than the first humans.

          —JANUARY 1946

This poem appeared first in the inaugural issue of *Chūgoku bunka*.

## WHEN WE SAY "HIROSHIMA"

When we say "Hiroshima,"
do people answer, gently,
"Ah, Hiroshima"?
Say "Hiroshima," and hear "Pearl Harbor."
Say "Hiroshima," and hear "Rape of Nanjing."
Say "Hiroshima," and hear of women and children in Manila
thrown into trenches, doused with gasoline,
and burned alive.
Say "Hiroshima,"
and hear echoes of blood and fire.

Say "Hiroshima,"
and we don't hear, gently,
"Ah, Hiroshima."
In chorus, Asia's dead and her voiceless masses
spit out the anger
of all those we made victims.
That we may say "Hiroshima,"
and hear in reply, gently,
"Ah, Hiroshima,"
we must in fact lay down
the arms we were supposed to lay down.
We must get rid of all foreign bases.
Until that day Hiroshima
will be a city of cruelty and bitter bad faith.
And we will be pariahs
burning with remnant radioactivity.

That we may say "Hiroshima"
and hear in reply, gently,

20

"Ah, Hiroshima,"
we first must
wash the blood
off our own hands.

—MAY 1972

# RIVER

### 1. Mountains and River

Majestic mountains linked one to the next,
mountain ranges spreading out
sharp, tall, heavy, large,
villages cut off from the sun by jagged mountains,
in deep shade even during the day,
beneath the fluttering wings of birds,
indigo blue headwaters—
      headwaters—
stream murmuring in meadows at the foot of mountains
and flowing through maple forests—
      flowing—
breaking over rocks and throwing up spray—
      throwing up spray,
spray falling back into the flow
and flowing on to eternal tomorrows.

### 2. River of Memory

Mirroring sky, mirroring mountains,
full of human joys and sorrows,
flowing, flowing,
from the distant, distant past,
strumming gently
the dawns and dusks of riverside villages—
O river where in our youth
we angled for carp and dace
and scooped red minnows from the shallows.
River flowing so clear,
sweetfish, silver arrows,

swimming in schools.
Living in a harsh world,
we long for the river—the river.
O river our mother!
O river! O river our mother!
O river our mother, tell us:
what is the meaning of life?

## 3. Flood

Cooled in its waters, cherries blossom, trees flourish
in villages along the river,
and the river flows gently—
    gently through riverside villages—
flows abundantly.
When sweetfish come downstream
and rice tassels form,
the sky will cloud over without warning:
a storm blowing up out of the south.
In the blink of an eye
the river turns muddy, rises,
and, snarling like a tornado,
rushes madly past;
eroding mountains, dashing against rocks,
the river roars crazily,
cuts dikes,
flows through paddy and field,
destroys every trace—every trace—of plant and tree.
The setting sun shines down
on people lingering in ruined villages,
the rice does not ripen,
the festival drums do not sound,
the villages are silent.

23

Cool, clear, the river rolls on—
    rolls on.

### 4. Dried-Up River

What is life?
Something without end, always moving forward.
The river, too, is a living thing
that has flowed for eons.
It does not stop, but the ships
that used to ply it are no more;
the white sails filled with wind—
dream? reality?
The water at the base of the mountains dries up—dries up,
and in the riverbed below the mountains,
river shrinks to rivulet.
What is that sound in the parched, parched riverbed—
frog? insect?

### 5. War

War—
vain undertaking
when blood flows like a river,
the flowing blood is sucked down into the sand,
and friend and foe join in mutual hate.
That day, too, the river flowed clear,
and as summer day began,
the brilliant light flashed:
instant of silence in which day turned to night,
buildings blew away,
and amid swirling flames
mother and child called to each other;
sky, river,

24

city
all burned—all burned.

## 6. River's Rebirth

Rain falls on the ruined city,
wind blows in the ruined city,
and white bones—bones—lie about like seashells.
Autumn comes to the ruined city,
plants regain color,
freshness;
river mirrors blue sky,
heals wounds;
bridges: arcs of steel suspended
over sevenfold river—river.
Peace Bridge, round suns of its handrails
conversing with the sun.
Flowing water mirrors dome;
eternal echo—
the mistake will not be repeated.
"In the twenty years since that day,
he passed on, and so did she.
At dawn I heard the faint sound of insects."
"Nights by the great river
are beautiful.
I'm glad I'm alive."
I'm glad I'm alive,
I'm glad I'm alive:
those who sang that tune—
they, too, are now dead.
O sevenfold river
flowing gently, slowly, through the city of rivers,
O current

creating our future once again.
Carry our joys and sorrows,
flow without cease,
flow forever,
forever, forever
without end.

—NOVEMBER 1966

RHM: The Ōta River that flows through Hiroshima splits into the seven rivers that Kurihara compares (in "City under Ground") to "a keloid hand opened out." On Kurihara's authority I have translated *gigira* "red minnow." Peace Bridge was designed by noted architect Tange Kenzō; its handrails end in sculpted discs representing the sun.

## THE HIROSHIMA NO ONE SERENADES

O Hiroshima
no one serenades—
turn a blind eye
to the charred scenes on the walls of the secret chamber,
    damp and dark,
and heave black sighs.
But the pain of that summer day
never fades.
Seek out the other Hiroshima,
fix it with a stare:
"Your eyes—
how can they be clear
as a summer lake?
I'd like
to gouge out your eyes
and get to the emptiness inside.
You and I—
we both were exposed to the flames.
I love you, I hate you."
O Hiroshima
no one serenades,
underneath the Hiroshima people do serenade.
Songs of Hiroshima born from its wounds
just as green trees stretch out branches
amid the rubble.
Serenades of Hiroshima
echo in the plaza,
the bloodsmeared faces of that summer day
never fade from the surface of the river. . . .

O sealed-off Hiroshima
no one serenades,
underneath the Hiroshima people do serenade—
refracting in my soul
and with that summer day
piercing my soul.
But
I sing—
for myself and for the other me.

—JULY 1960

RHM: The secret chamber with scenes on the wall of nuclear destruction is a metaphor for the grim, enclosed world of the *hibakusha*. Kurihara sets that Hiroshima against the Hiroshima of glittering modern buildings and has the two converse. In the final stanza, the poet reenters the picture.

# I BEAR WITNESS FOR HIROSHIMA

As a survivor, I wish first of all
to be a human being,
and all the more, as one mother,
I would weep over them now, while they are alive,
the tears I'd shed over their corpses
should the clear skies above these red-cheeked infants
and everyone else
suddenly one day rip open
and condemn many to be burned alive.
Above all, I oppose war,
and even if they try under one label or another to punish
a mother's saying no to her children's death,
I will not flee or hide,
for that day's hell
is seared onto my retinas.

August sixth, 1945:
the sun rose, and soon
people set gravely about their daily rounds;
suddenly
the city was blown away,
skin blistered,
the seven rivers filled with corpses.

The tale goes
that if those who get a look at hell talk of hell,
hell's devil-king will call them back,
but as a survivor, witness for Hiroshima,
I testify wherever I go,
and even if it should cost me my life, I sing,
"An end to war!"

—SEPTEMBER 1952

# Transition

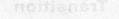

## IN THE MIDST OF DESTRUCTION

In the rubble a single wildflower
sent out small white blossoms.
From the burned soil filled with the bones
of fathers, mothers, brothers, relatives,
from the now-silent ruins
where every living thing burned to death:
a small life that taught us to live.
Hiroshima, carrying on from that day—
a flower blooming in the midst of destruction.

—MARCH 1988

# Part Two

Part Two

## THE FLAG, I

As if nothing at all had gone wrong,
the flag fluttered once more
high over the roofs
and began to dream again of carnage in broad daylight.
But no one looked up to it,
and people resented its insatiable greed
and gnashed their teeth at its monstrous amnesia.

Beneath that flag
each morning,
dizzy from malnutrition,
we were made to swear the oath of slaves
and, waving that flag, send off
fathers and brothers
wearing red sashes.
Ever since it flew over ramparts on the continent,
that flag has believed fanatically in the dream of empire.
From far Guadalcanal
to the cliffs of Corregidor.
It drove our fathers and husbands
into the caves of Iwojima and Saipan,
starved them like wild beasts,
and scattered their white bones.

Ah! Red-on-white flag of Japan!
The many nightmarish atrocities carried out at your feet.
Manila and Nanjing, where they splashed gasoline
        over women and children
and burned them alive—
consummate crimes of the twentieth century.

Yet today the flag flutters again, shameless,
all those bloody memories
gone;
fluttering, fluttering in the breeze,
it dreams once more of redrawing the map.

—JUNE 1952

RHM: Shortly after the surrender, Japan's Ministry of Education prohibited the flying of the flag. General MacArthur eased the prohibition in 1947, allowed the flag to be flown on holidays in 1948, and abolished all restrictions in his New Year's message of 1950.

# JAPAN'S WINTER OF 1961

And now
dark winter comes to the islands of Japan;
particles the eye can't see
fall onto petals of chrysanthemums still in bloom,
onto leaves still clinging to roadside trees;
they fall
onto the soft hair of children,
onto the shoulders and backs of farm women in the fields,
soundlessly, they fall
onto city buildings,
into island rain barrels,
they fall
onto the cenotaph in Peace Park,
onto the grassy mound over the mass grave,
and the patients in the atomic hospital shake with terror.

The sea of banners that surged
under the June sun has receded,
the voices from Niijima and Miho that sang out so
have rippled away,
and onto the islands of Japan
particles the eye can't see
continue to fall.

—NOVEMBER 1961

RHM: Niijima and Miho were locations for missile sites and places of note
in the summer 1960 demonstrations against the U.S.-Japan Security Treaty.

39

## EXPOSURE

I wear blue, like a prison uniform.
A woman in white asks me to open wide
and, as if feeding livestock,
shoves white medicine from a tube down my throat.

I press my chest
to an upright white stand,
and the x-ray camera
clicks.
Radiation passes through my body.

The white stand falls forward,
and now, face down,
I'm told
to hold my breath and lie on my right side,
on my left, on my back.
I obey, and each time the x-ray camera clicks
and radiation passes through my body.

I wonder how much of the radiation
I received with the flash and blast that summer
is still inside me.
Is its half-life over?
Black forebodings flit across my mind:
damaged genes, chromosomes,
children with congenital defects.

The white stand returns to upright,
and I'm back where I began.
I turn to the right,

and in front of me is another white stand.
As if in an oil press,
I'm squeezed and squashed
from front and back.
Under the eye of a video camera,
I drink white fluid, a sort of sludge,
from a large cup.

Holding my breath,
I turn left, turn right.
Each time the machine clicks,
and radiation passes through my body.

The data:
is it entered
into the ABCC's computer
and sent to the United States?
The ABCC continues even now
to pursue *hibakusha*;
from atop the hill,
it overlooks all the hospitals in the city.

—DECEMBER 1977

41

## NIPPON: PIROSHIMA

### I

The mayor of Piroshima
is an old fox
who likes to dress up in tuxedos.
Pulling on white gloves,
he gives speeches larded with English,
"*Piisu.*" "*Piisu.*"

The mayor of Piroshima
constructs a zoo
in Piroshima's back parlor,
invites rare beasts from all over the world,
and opens it to the public on August sixth.

August sixth, see,
is the day 200,000 people of Hiroshima
were broiled to death by rays,
the day the seven rivers filled with corpses,
the day a great swarm of people fled,
torn flesh hanging,
and died in agony by the road.

For the mayor of Piroshima,
August sixth is a grand memorial service for blowfish.
This—the day that commemorates the corpses with torn flesh
        piled up,
soaked with gasoline, cremated.
May their souls find rest. "*Piisu.*" "*Piisu.*"

His address goes out via radio
to the whole world.
A grand, grand ceremony.

To please the children,
he trots out a two-humped camel and a black rhino,
and to scare the adults
he summons
from Tokyo
a bug-eyed monster
to give a speech from the dais.
Nippon: Piroshima—
Ha. Ha. Ha.

### 2

The mayor of Piroshima
is an old fox
who likes to dress up in tuxedos.
Pulling on white gloves,
he gives speeches larded with English,
"Piisu." "Piisu."

Several years ago
the mayor of Piroshima wanted to rebuild
Piroshima's old Supreme Command,
so that it and the atomic dome could coexist.
On the great *torii* of the shrine
     where the Supreme Command once stood
you can see even now the name of its donor,
     Lieutenant General so-and-so.

43

In the summer,
the mayor of Piroshima stands before
     the saddle-shaped cenotaph,
has the bells rung and the doves released,
and reads his address.
"The mistake will not be repeated."
"Piisu." "Piisu."
In the fall
he reviews the line of heavy tanks and artillery
that rushes ahead toward the fourth five-year plan
and tramples on the layers of human bones
     beneath the cenotaph.
At that time the mayor of Piroshima
becomes the mayor of Fortress Hiroshima
and strikes a pose.


The mayor of Piroshima
is an old priest
in love with ceremonies.
The ceremony marking the twenty-sixth anniversary of the
     bomb,
the twenty-first annual review of the troops—
the same
high ceremony.
"The Self-Defense Force is not an army."
"Ours is a peace constitution,
so this is not militarism."
"Small-scale nuclear weapons
are not unconstitutional."
Nippon: Piroshima.
Nippon: Piroshima.

The old priest in love with ceremonies
will ceremony Hiroshima
to death.

—OCTOBER 1971

Part 1 of the poem was written in August 1971; part 2 in October 1971. The summer of 1971 marked Prime Minister Sato's first ceremonial visit to the atomic cenotaph.

RHM: The title of this poem in Japanese is *Nippon: Piroshima*, written phonetically in *katakana* rather than characters. *Nippon*, the harsher pronunciation of *Nihon*, "Japan," carries connotations of the war and militarism. *Piroshima* looks exactly like Hiroshima except that a small circle above the *Hi* turns it into the aspirated *Pi*. In the poem Kurihara moves from the aspirated *pon* of *Nippon*, to the *Pi* of *Piroshima*, to the *pi* of *piisu*, a phonetic representation of the English "peace," line 6. The strange beasts in stanza 2 presumably are VIPs from abroad. Blowfish are a culinary delight, the taste reinforced by the danger involved—improperly prepared blowfish livers are fatal. A service for blowfish would thank them for their usefulness to humankind, beg their forgiveness for humankind's use of them, and ask their forbearance in the future. The reference to blowfish resonates in at least two ways: its utter inconsequence compared with 6 August and a parallel with 6 August—the agony that blowfish poisoning causes its victims and the agony of atomic bomb deaths. Sato Eisaku, prime minister from 1964 to 1972, was a former Class A war crimes suspect. He was also a caricaturist's delight: heavy eyebrows and large eyes. Hiroshima's Supreme Command, a structure set up on the grounds of Hiroshima Castle and made use of only in time of war, served its intended purpose during the Russo-Japanese War; it was destroyed on 6 August.

45

# THE CHERRY TREES OF HIROSHIMA

On the riverbanks
in the park,
cherry blossoms bloom like cotton candy,
and people climb down from tourist buses
to face the tombstone that swells like the back
    of a dead horse
and snap their snapshots.
She poses
with the abstract monument
as backdrop—
and doesn't the blue light suddenly flash?
The monument's mother, babe, and small daughters—
aren't they blown to smithereens?
The cherries in full blossom like cotton candy—
don't they turn to flame, swirl inside the park,
and, crossing the river,
collide with flames on the other side?
Doesn't the river flow straight up into the sky,
become a cyclone,
and take people and trees and buildings
high up into the air?

The naked dead who crowded together that day
on the granite slopes of the riverbank
sank into the cold river,
and in the eyes of the dead
the cherries blossoming palely like cotton candy
still appear the color of flame.
This year, too, the cherry trees in the park
intertwine their branches, and the road along the river

is a bright arcade of flowers.
But this season in Japan
is a season of bitter demonstrations—
young people, eyes overflowing from the shroud
of tear gas, throwing rocks.
It is a season of the blood of young people
with broken skulls.
It is a season of flames
when the cherry trees inside the barricades
suddenly blaze up.

—JULY 1969

RHM: The abstract monument is not the cenotaph but a sculpture by Hongō Shin (1905–80). Titled "Mother and Children in the Tempest" (1953), it is situated on the southern edge of Peace Park.

## OUT OF THE STONE

Out of the stone they sound,
the voices of the tens of thousands who burned to death.
Charged with age-old bitter feelings,
they fill the night air.
*Mul! Mul talla! Mul talla!*
Water! Water, please! Water, please!

From the riverbank monument
for which there was no room in Peace Park,
all night long, they come, the voices
        of the tens of thousands dead:
*Mul! Mul talla! Mul talla!*

Rounded up
as they tilled the soil of Korean fields,
rounded up
as they walked the streets
of Korean towns and villages,
not allowed to say even a word of farewell
to wives and children, parents, brothers, sisters,
they were packed like livestock into transports
and shipped off, across the strait.

Forced to pray to foreign gods,
to swear allegiance to a foreign ruler,
in the end burned in that flash, they were turned
        into black corpses
for swarms of crows to peck at.

*Aigu! Mul! Mul talla!*
The homeland was torn in two,

48

and one torn half was forced to house
thousands of atomic weapons.
Why should the atom be forced
on us and our half?
Leave, you foreign soldiers!
Take your atomic bombs, and leave!
The homeland is one.
O Wind, take the message—that out of the stone
this torn half calls out to its own kind.

—JULY 1980

RHM: Hiroshima's memorial to the thousands of Koreans who died on 6
August is outside Peace Park, at the western end of one of the bridges. The
strait is Tsushima Strait, which separates Korea and Japan; *aigu* is an excla-
mation of woe.

49

## THE DAY THE SHŌWA ERA ENDS

Deep inside the moat on which swans drift, oblivious,
the emperor is in pain,
now vomiting blood, now passing blood,
only dimly conscious.
Does he think of them?

Victims of the atomic bomb
lying on straw in sheds and stables
of the farms to which they fled
that summer's day forty-three years ago,
ridden with fever, trembling from chills,
breaking out all over in red spots,
hair falling out, no medical treatment of any kind,
not knowing even the name of their affliction,
who died with blood pouring from ears, mouths, noses;
victims of the atomic bomb who passed
        so much blood their bowels seemed to have melted,
who hadn't even rags to use as diapers,
who died drowning in blood.

Rallying with transfusion after transfusion,
hardly conscious,
does he mount his white horse
and wander distant battlefields?
The hell of starvation in island jungles
        of countries to the south,
on the cliffs of the continent,
that made people eat snakes, frogs, human flesh.
Soldiers wracked by malarial fevers,
shivering from chills

beneath the sizzling southern sun,
arms and legs blown away by naval artillery,
unable even to move,
who died on foreign soil—
as his life ebbs,
does he make a tour of inspection?


A single life should count more than the world;
one life should count for no more
than any other.
Yet counting for less than a feather,
those husbands and sons went to their deaths singing,
"At sea be my corpse water-soaked;
　　　on land let grass grow over it.
Let me die beside my lord."
Their one-time lord—while wandering the borderland
　　　between life and death,
does he make his way
to the battlefields of Greater East Asia
to hand out imperial gift cigarettes
and award Orders of the Golden Kite?


Even after the war ended
the one-time commander-in-chief
never showed contrition for his sins.
Will the Greater East Asian war finally come to an end
on the day the Shōwa era ends?
Or does Japan stand already
on the threshold of new war?
The voices of the cicadas that cried bitterly all over Japan

in August forty-three years ago
resound now,
deafeningly loud.

—DECEMBER 1988

RHM: This poem was Kurihara's contribution to an anthology of the same title, a collection of hostile poems composed during the Shōwa emperor's final illness. The quotation comes from *Kokinshū*.

## I SAW HIROSHIMA

You saw nothing in Hiroshima.
Hiroshima: city of buildings and cars.
Couples in blue jeans snooze
on benches in the park,
a small child frolics with the pigeons on the grass.
The atomic dome,
the cenotaph—
they're only backdrops for snapshots.

No, this is what I saw.
People sitting in a group, like ascetics,
on the pavement in front of the cenotaph.
Moving not at all
and silent,
tuned into underground nuclear tests
in the deserts of far, far countries
and the soundless sound
of death ash blowing overhead,
people who once saw atomic hell.
People sitting on the pavement
and conversing with the dead,
joining with the dead
to call for peace.

This is what I saw.
People in Hiroshima
sitting on the pavement
and calling for peace.

—November 1977

53

## HIROSHIMA, AUSCHWITZ:
## WE MUST NOT FORGET

What Auschwitz left behind:
mounds of striped inmate uniforms, children's small shoes,
and girls' red ribbons,
eating bowls that served also as chamber pots,
soap made from human fat,
cloth woven of human hair.

What Auschwitz left behind:
turn all the world's blue skies and seas into ink
and there still wouldn't be enough
        to express the sadness, the anger,
the moans of those burned in the ovens.

What Hiroshima and Nagasaki left behind:
a human shape burned onto stone,
black rain streaking a wall,
radioactivity inside bodies,
microcephalic babies irradiated in the womb,
voices of the dead sounding from the skies,
voices of the dead sounding from the bowels of the earth.

Hiroshima, Auschwitz: we must not forget.
Nagasaki, Auschwitz: we must not forget.
Even if the first time was a mistake,
the second time will be calculated malice.
The vow we made to the dead: we must not forget.

—DECEMBER 1989

54

## SHADES: THE POST-DOOMSDAY WORLD

The world sinks toward evening;
in the ashen sky
shades drift, drift in the wind.
Dawn, dawn:
it will not come again.

Flowers
trees
butterflies
birds
cats
dogs
human beings:
all living things, not to be born again,
become mere shades
trembling like ribbons,
shrinking like balloons,
bursting like bubbles.
Without a word of resentment
they drift, drift in the wind.
Dawn: it will not come again.
Dawn: it will not come again.

—OCTOBER 1971

55

## PRAYER FOR A NUCLEAR-FREE TOMORROW
—For Kazuko


The forty-fourth August is here,
and the field of rubble
has become a city of gleaming buildings
ablaze in the summer sun.
The last structures from that time vanish
one by one,
and atomic bomb sites
become myths of Hiroshima man.

The drama of birth at the dawn of the atomic era,
in the hellish dark basement
of a shattered building,
has been engraved on the monument
to be unveiled August sixth.
To unveil the monument:
she who was born in that basement.
The mother who gave birth,
the midwife who helped with the birth,
the people who forgot their own pains to assist them—
they have all
departed this world.

But she who was born
at the very moment of the bomb
has become the mother of a dear child,

and with a prayer for a nuclear-free tomorrow,
she unveils a new age.

—JULY 1989

RHM: Kazuko is Kojima Kazuko. The building that Kurihara's poem "Let Us Be Midwives!" made famous was razed in 1988. On 6 August 1989 a monument was dedicated; the monument includes a photograph of the old building and the full text of "Let Us Be Midwives!"

Printed and bound by CPI Group (UK) Ltd, Croydon, CR0 4YY

13/04/2025

14656528-0001